Major European Union Nations

Austria
Belgium
Czech Republic
Denmark
France
Germany
Greece
Ireland

Italy
The Netherlands
Poland
Portugal
Spain
Sweden
United Kingdom

Major European
Union Nations

PORTUGAL

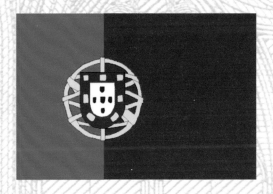

by
Kim Etingoff and Shaina C. Indovino

Mason Crest

Mason Crest
370 Reed Road, Broomall,
Pennsylvania 19008
www.masoncrest.com

Printed in the Hashemite Kingdom of Jordan.

First printing
9 8 7 6 5 4 3 2 1

Library of Congress Cataloging-in-Publication Data

Etingoff, Kim.
   Portugal / by Kim Etingoff and Shaina C. Indovino.
      p. cm. — (The European Union: political, social, and economic cooperation)
   Includes bibliographical references and index.
   ISBN 978-1-4222-2255-3 (hardcover) — ISBN 978-1-4222-2231-7 (series hardcover) — ISBN 978-1-4222-9273-0 (ebook)
   I. Indovino, Shaina Carmel. II. Title.
   DP517.E842 2012
   946.9—dc22
                                        2010051466

Produced by Harding House Publishing Services, Inc.
www.hardinghousepages.com
Interior layout by Micaela Sanna.
Cover design by Torque Advertising + Design.

Contents

PORTUGAL
European Union Member since 1986

Chaves

Braga

Vila do Conde

Vila Real

Porto

Aveiro

Viseu

Guarda

Coimbra

Figueira da Foz

Castelo Branco

Portalegre

Santarém

Lisbon

Almada

Setúbal

Evora

Beja

Portiãmo

Faro

Olhão

INTRODUCTION

Sixty years ago, Europe lay scarred from the battles of the Second World War. During the next several years, a plan began to take shape that would unite the countries of the European continent so that future wars would be inconceivable. On May 9, 1950, French Foreign Minister Robert Schuman issued a declaration calling on France, Germany, and other European countries to pool together their coal and steel production as "the first concrete foundation of a European federation." "Europe Day" is celebrated each year on May 9 to commemorate the beginning of the European Union (EU).

The EU consists of twenty-seven countries, spanning the continent from Ireland in the west to the border of Russia in the east. Eight of the ten most recently admitted EU member states are former communist regimes that were behind the Iron Curtain for most of the latter half of the twentieth century.

Any European country with a democratic government, a functioning market economy, respect for fundamental rights, and a government capable of implementing EU laws and policies may apply for membership. Bulgaria and Romania joined the EU in 2007. Croatia, Serbia, Turkey, Iceland, Montenegro, and Macedonia have also embarked on the road to EU membership.

While the EU began as an idea to ensure peace in Europe through interconnected economies, it has evolved into so much more today:

- Citizens can travel freely throughout most of the EU without carrying a passport and without stopping for border checks.

- EU citizens can live, work, study, and retire in another EU country if they wish.

- The euro, the single currency accepted throughout seventeen of the EU countries (with more to come), is one of the EU's most tangible achievements, facilitating commerce and making possible a single financial market that benefits both individuals and businesses.

- The EU ensures cooperation in the fight against cross-border crime and terrorism.

- The EU is spearheading world efforts to preserve the environment.

- As the world's largest trading bloc, the EU uses its influence to promote fair rules for world trade, ensuring that globalization also benefits the poorest countries.

- The EU is already the world's largest donor of humanitarian aid and development assistance, providing around 60 percent of global official development assistance to developing countries in 2011.

The EU is not a nation intended to replace existing nations. The EU is unique—its member countries have established common institutions to which they delegate some of their sovereignty so that decisions on matters of joint interest can be made democratically at the European level.

Europe is a continent with many different traditions and languages, but with shared values such as democracy, freedom, and social justice, cherished values well known to North Americans. Indeed, the EU motto is "United in Diversity."

Enjoy your reading. Take advantage of this chance to learn more about Europe and the EU!

Ambassador John Bruton,
Former EU President and Prime Minister of Ireland

Marco Polo Bridge in
Lisbon, Portugal.

1 CHAPTER

PORTUGAL'S MODERN ISSUES

In recent years, Portugal is often overshadowed by its larger neighbor, Spain. However, it was once a wealthy and powerful nation, owning an empire that stretched across the globe. Although the country has lost much of that glory, Portugal remains a colorful and fascinating country in modern times.

The EU unites European nations.

Portugal joined the European Union (EU), then known as the European Economic Community (EEC), in 1986. At the time, several member countries, including the UK, France, and Germany, were worried about taking on the problems of a poorer nation like Portugal. With EU membership, Portugal was given financial aid that was meant to help its economy grow and to ease its social problems. Portugal needed that money to meet the standards the EU set for membership.

Portugal used the EU aid to improve its *infrastructure*. Money went to things like roads, communications, hospitals, and schools. Thanks to this

THE FORMATION OF THE EUROPEAN UNION

The EU is a confederation of European nations that continues to grow. All countries that enter the EU agree to follow common laws about foreign security policies. They also agree to cooperate on legal matters that go on within the EU. The European Council meets to discuss all international matters and make decisions about them. Each country's own concerns and interests are important, though. And apart from legal and financial issues, the EU tries to uphold values such as peace and solidarity, human dignity, freedom, and equality. All member countries remain autonomous. This means that they generally keep their own laws and regulations. The EU becomes involved only if there is an international issue or if a member country has violated the principles of the union.

The idea for a union among European nations was first mentioned after World War II. The war had devastated much of Europe, both physically and financially. In 1950, French foreign minister Robert Schuman suggested that France and West Germany combine their coal and steel industries under one authority. Both countries would have control over the industries. This would help them become more financially stable. It would also make war between the countries much more difficult. The idea was interesting to other European countries as well. In 1951, France, West Germany, Belgium, Luxembourg, the Netherlands, and Italy signed the Treaty of Paris, creating the European Coal and Steel Community. These six countries would become the core of the EU.

In 1957, these same countries signed the Treaties of Rome, creating the European Economic Community. This combined their economies into a single European economy. In 1965, the Merger Treaty brought together a number of these treaty organizations. The organizations were joined under a common banner, known as the European Community. Finally, in 1992, the Maastricht Treaty was signed. This treaty defined the European Union. It gave a framework for expanding the EU's political role, particularly in the area of foreign and security policy. It would also replace national currencies with the euro. The next year, the treaty went into effect. At that time, the member countries included the original six plus another six who had joined during the 1970s and '80s.

In the following years, the EU would take more steps to form a single market for its members. This would make joining the union even more of an advantage. Three more countries joined during the 1990s. Another twelve joined in the first decade of the twenty-first century. As of 2012, six countries were waiting to join the EU.

assistance, Portugal was slowly able to achieve a much more stable economy that continued to grow until the early years of the twenty-first century.

Then in 2008, a global recession—a time of serious **economic** slowdown—spread around the world. Businesses stopped growing or went out of business altogether. Many people were out of work. In the European Union, Portugal was one of the countries hit the hardest by the recession. And as a result of the recession, twenty-first-century Portugal is facing a host of new issues.

POLITICS

Like much of the EU, modern Portugal is a **socialist** nation. This means that the government pays for many social welfare services, such as health care and **pension** benefits. But the recession plunged Portugal's government deep into debt. Its budget **deficit** was greater than what the EU allows its members to have while being part of the eurozone (the area that uses the euro as its currency).

Prime Minister José Sócrates proposed an **austerity** plan to help get his nation's finances back on track. Sócrates was a **liberal** politician who wanted to make many **progressive** changes to his country's laws, including the legalization of same-sex marriages—but the liberal voters who would normally have supported Sócrates were angry about the cutbacks he had made to social services.

Pedro Passos Coelho became the prime minister of Portugal in 2011.

WHO ARE THE ROMA?

About a thousand years ago, groups of people migrated from northern India, spreading across Europe over the next several centuries. Though these people actually came from several different tribes (the largest of which were the Sinti and Roma), the people of Europe called them simply "Gypsies"—a shortened version of "Egyptians," since people thought they came from Egypt.

Europeans were frightened of these dark-skinned, non-Christian people who spoke a foreign language. Unlike the settled people of Europe, the Roma were wanderers, with no ties to the land. Europeans did not understand them. Stories and stereotypes grew about the Gypsies, and these fanned the flames of prejudice and discrimination. Many of these same stories and stereotypes are still believed today.

Throughout the centuries, non-Gypsies continually tried to either assimilate the Gypsies or kill them. Attempts to assimilate the Gypsies involved stealing their children and placing them with other families; giving them cattle and feed, expecting them to become farmers; outlawing their customs, language, and clothing, and forcing them to attend school and church. In many ways the Roma of Europe were treated much as the European settlers treated the Native peoples of North America.

Many European laws allowed—or even commanded—the killing of Gypsies. A practice of "Gypsy hunting"—similar to fox hunting—was both common and legal in some parts of Europe. Even as late as 1835, a Gypsy hunt in Denmark "brought in a bag of over 260 men, women, and children." But the worst of all crimes against the Roma happened in the twentieth century, when Hitler's Third Reich sent them to concentration camps. As many as half a million Roma died in the Nazis' death camps.

These issues have led to a political battle in Portugal between the liberal Socialist Party and the more **conservative** Social Democratic Party. Polls showed that voters were split nearly evenly between these two sides. And some Portuguese were so tired of the situation that they were ready to leave their country altogether.

EMIGRATION

Portugal's economic crisis is driving thousands of young people to look for work in other countries. These **emigrants** are mostly young university graduates or skilled technicians who lack work opportunities in their homeland. Many of them are moving to Brazil—where the economic atmosphere is far more hopeful—or to countries in Africa and Asia that, like Brazil, were once Portuguese colonies. Less-skilled emigrants—truck drivers, construction workers, and electricians—are heading to Angola in southwest Africa. Angola's oil and diamonds have made its economy one of the fastest growing in the world.

Over the past years, Portugal's government has spent millions of dollars on educating its young people, in the hopes that its professionals will be

Traditional Gypsy homes.

able to compete with the rest of the world—and now all that money is leaving the country. Young Portuguese professionals feel at home in Portugal's former colonies, where Portuguese is the official language—and when their homeland can offer them neither jobs nor unemployment benefits, they feel they have nothing to lose by leaving. Meanwhile, though, Portugal will have a hard time recovering from their loss.

HUMAN RIGHTS

With so many people in Portugal facing economic hardship, many Portuguese resent the presence of a group of people who have been living in poverty for centuries—the Roma. There are between 40,000 and 50,000 Roma who live in Portugal, and they often face **prejudice** and **discrimination**.

Many Portuguese Roma lack education, and they often live in unhealthy slums. In the 1990s, the Portuguese government began working to provide better housing for the Roma, but the recession and the government's austerity measures have meant that many of these programs are no longer funded.

Researchers have found that the Roma—referred to as "Ciganos" in Portugal—are the group that the Portuguese most reject and discriminate against. Many local governments refuse to allow the Roma access to job placement and housing services, and the police often treat them unfairly.

Meanwhile, the EU has committed itself to improving the lives of the Roma throughout Europe. This, combined with Portugal needing so much funding from the EU to help it with its financial problems, has cast a shadow across the reputation of this once rich and respected nation.

2 PORTUGAL'S HISTORY AND GOVERNMENT

Portugal has a long, rich history that begins in prehistoric times and spans many centuries. Its history has helped shape Portugal's culture and who its people are today.

Early Portugal

Scientists have speculated that people have inhabited Portugal for the past 500,000 years. **Hunter-gatherers**, who lived along river valleys, were the main residents for much of the earliest part of this time. Advanced settlements—fortified villages in the Tagus Valley—have been discovered that date back to 5500 BCE.

In 700 BCE, the peninsula was settled by a group of people known as the Celts, who arrived

Visigoths, a Germanic tribe, conquered almost all the peninsula in the fifth century CE. These invaders came from the area around what is now Germany.

The Golden Age of the Moors and Christian Reconquest

The Moors, a group of Arabic peoples, were one of the most important influences on the Iberian Peninsula. Arriving from northern Africa, they began their occupation of present-day Portugal and Spain in 711 CE. They conquered most of the peninsula, except for one small piece of land in the northwest.

The Moors left a lasting mark on Portugal that is still evident today, especially in the Algarve in the south, which the Moors preferred to the rest of the country because of its hot, dry conditions that reminded them of their homelands. Their centuries-long inhabitance of the area, referred to as al-Andalus by the Moors, meant that the cultures of the Moors and the local Portuguese natives

Dating Systems and Their Meaning

You might be accustomed to seeing dates expressed with the abbreviations BC or AD, as in the year 1000 BC or the year AD 1900. For centuries, this dating system has been the most common in the Western world. However, since BC and AD are based on Christianity (BC stands for Before Christ and AD stands for *anno Domini*, Latin for "in the year of our Lord"), many people now prefer to use abbreviations that people from all religions can be comfortable using. The abbreviations BCE (meaning Before Common Era) and CE (meaning Common Era) mark time in the same way (for example, 1000 BC is the same year as 1000 BCE, and AD 1900 is the same year as 1900 CE), but BCE and CE do not have the same religious overtones as BC and AD.

from Central Europe. They **assimilated** into the local culture of the people already living in the area, forming the Celt-Iberians, or Lusitanians. Many other groups followed, including the Phoenicians, Greeks, and Romans, who first invaded the peninsula in 219 BCE. The

mixed together, forming a unique blend of customs, architecture, food, and language that can only be found on the Iberian Peninsula.

Under the Moors, peace and prosperity were brought to Portugal. Most of the natives were easily converted to Islam, although religious toleration

The Castle of Ourem

EUROPEAN UNION—PORTUGAL

was practiced. Education, the arts, and industry all leaped ahead, transforming Portugal into a center of culture and trade.

The occupation of the Moors ended in the eleventh century. Power-hungry Moorish nobles divided the empire between themselves, providing an opportunity for Visigothic Christians who had remained unconquered to retake the peninsula. Slowly, Christian nobles were able to regain control over the Moors, although fighting was ongoing for over two hundred years.

THE FORMATION OF PORTUGAL

The king of Astúrias-León, who had gained power after fighting the Moors, appointed nobles to rule the province of Portucalense. Soon, rule over this area became a **hereditary** title. One count, Afonso Henriques, proclaimed himself king of Portugal and was eventually recognized by the king of Astúrias-León in 1143.

Afonso Henriques and his heirs conquered the remaining Muslims, and over the period of about a century, they expanded the borders of the kingdom to form what is now the familiar shape of Portugal.

EXPANSION

In the fifteenth century, Portugal began to explore the oceans and beyond, ushering in a period of glory. The need for new trade routes, as well as the fact that the country had expanded as far as it could on the Iberian Peninsula, meant that Portugal had to look to the seas. Portugal also had advanced nautical knowledge and a good position for naval exploration.

The major force behind Portugal's exploration was Prince Henry the Navigator, the son of King João (John). Under his direction and financial help, the ships of Portugal were able to create new trade routes and a new empire. At its greatest extent, the empire reached India, Brazil, and Africa.

During the 1400s, Portugal was one of the most powerful countries in the world. The monarchy became the richest in Europe, and they established the country as a center for trade.

THE INQUISITION

Despite the prosperity that Portugal seemed to have, many problems lurked beneath the surface. Social inequality continued, and freedom of speech was not encouraged. One of the most famous examples of this is the Inquisition. This repression of freedom of religion took place in Portugal, as well as in Spain.

In 1539, the king of Portugal, João III, set up a Court of Inquisition, which tried and condemned 1,400 people to death for **heresy**. Many of those sentenced to death were Jews who had already converted to Christianity, but who were suspected of still practicing Judaism.

THE DECLINE OF PORTUGAL

The empire's wealth and power depended on the strength of the monarch. After the death of João

Bragança Palace

III, who had been a powerful king, Portugal's glory declined because of the lack of another strong king.

In 1580, Spain invaded and **annexed** Portugal, making Spain's Phillip II, who was crowned Felipe I, king of Portugal. Under Spain, the country became too weak to hold on to its empire, so it lost much of the land it had held in Asia and Africa. Portugal was able to regain its independence in 1640, but not its former power.

DEMOCRACY TAKES HOLD

As in other European countries, **republicanism** became a widespread idea in Portugal in the 1800s. The recent French Revolution helped to spread the desire for democracy, as did **propaganda** that made its way into Portugal. In 1812, a secret society, the Sinédrio, was formed to pass on revolutionary ideas.

In 1822, a constitutional monarchy was created. While the king still held power, he shared it with a legislative body (the Chamber of Deputies) and a court system. This new constitution created a division in society between those who supported it and those who wanted to go back to a complete monarchy.

Later, another constitution, the Constitutional Charter, was created, giving the king more power. However, in 1828, King Miguel I declared that this constitution was **null**. A later king, Pedro II, restored it. In 1910, the monarchy was completely abolished after many demonstrations and unrest,

and a democratic republic was set up in a blood-less revolution.

PROBLEMS WITH DEMOCRACY

For the next fifteen years, Portugal had a troubled and unstable government. The outbreak of World War I did not help the struggling country. In 1916, 40,000 Portuguese forces were sent to fight with the Allies. Unfortunately, they were not well trained or well equipped, and many of the men were killed in the fighting. Learning from its mistakes, Portugal remained neutral in World War II. However, it allowed the Allies to build air and naval bases on Portuguese territory.

Three attempts were made to overthrow the government after democracy was established. One, in 1926, led to dictatorship under António de Oliveira Salazar. His reign was not as oppressive as others of the time, and even included some improvements on society, such as giving women the right to vote. However, people were still unable to freely express their opinions, and all political parties were banned. Salazar's government ended with his death in 1968.

Under Salazar, Portugal's economy grew very slowly. By the middle of the twentieth century, the country was clearly behind those of the rest of Europe and was admitted late to the United Nations, in 1955. After Salazar's death, a successful revolt **deposed** his successor, Marcello Caetano, and set up a new, democratic government.

There was also unrest in many of Portugal's remaining colonies, especially those in Africa.

CHAPTER TWO 29

Portugal lost money dealing with revolts and wars, eventually ending in independence for all of Portugal's colonies in 1974 and 1975.

MODERN PORTUGAL

Over the last few decades, Portugal has slowly recovered some of its lost power and has entered the global community. In 1986, the country joined the European Community, which would eventually become the European Union (EU). It also became a member of the European Monetary Union in 1999.

The current government is much more stable than it has been in the past. The president is elected every five years and can appoint the prime minister. The Council of Ministers makes up the rest of the executive branch. The legislative body is made up the 230-member Assembly of the Republic, a **unicameral** house. The government also includes a court system, with the Supreme Court being the highest court. The government has been working hard in recent years to improve the country's economy.

But the Portuguese people do not always like their government's efforts to heal their nation's economy. When the government put into effect three rounds of austerity measures, Portuguese workers were angry. Meanwhile, the nation continued to plunge deeper and deeper into its economic crisis. That crisis led to the resignation of Prime Minister José Sócrates, after opposition parties rejected his last-ditch attempt to push through a fourth package of spending cuts and tax increases. Mr. Sócrates stayed on, leading a caretaker government until June 2011, when his Socialist party was soundly defeated in the elections. Pedro Passos Coelho, the leader of the Social Democrats, became prime minister then. But Portugal's economic problems continued, with no easy answers in sight for the people of this ancient nation.

Portugal's beaches draw tourists who contribute to the nation's economy.

3 CHAPTER THE ECONOMY

Portugal has become a **diversified** and increasingly **service-based** economy since joining the European Community in 1986. The country qualified to become a part of the eurozone in 1998 and began circulating the euro on January 1, 2002.

During the 1990s, the economy grew faster than the EU average but that began to change in 2001, and then in 2009, Portugal's economy began to **contract**. The **gross domestic product (GDP) per capita** is now about two-thirds of the average for the rest of the EU.

AGRICULTURE

In today's world, most countries have begun to rely less and less on farming to sustain their economies. Portugal's economy, on the other hand, still relies heavily on agriculture. About 12 percent of the population is involved with farming, forestry, or fishing, and around one quarter of the land on continental Portugal is used for the growing of crops. Most of that land grows olives, wheat, corn, grapes, potatoes, and tomatoes. Fruits, especially citrus fruits like oranges, are also grown.

The products made from these crops are sold throughout the world, as well as locally in Portugal. Portuguese wines and olive oils are especially well known.

A Portuguese shepherd and his flock.

Despite the number of people and land dedicated to agriculture, it provides Portugal with less than 3 percent of its gross domestic product (GDP). This is because not enough modern technology is used to get the most out of agriculture. The solution to this problem is one of Portugal's long-term goals.

GROWING INDUSTRY AND TRADE

Manufacturing and industry have grown in Portugal during the twentieth and twenty-first centuries, especially after it joined the EU. Although it still tends to lag behind other Western European countries, it is slowly establishing itself in industries such as automobile production, electronics, paper manufacturing, and food processing.

Portugal trades mostly with other EU member states. It imports most of its products from EU members such as Spain, Italy, Germany, and France. It exports its products to Germany, France, and Spain. Portugal's primary exports are agricultural goods, taking advantage of its supply of cork trees, other wood, and fruit. It imports machinery, cars, oil, and textiles.

NATURAL RESOURCES

One of Portugal's largest resources is wood. Portugal alone provides the world with over half of its supply of cork oak wood. About 36 percent of the land, par-

Buçaco Palace in the midst of Portugal's forests

ticularly in the north, is covered in trees, including pine trees, holm oak, cork oak, and eucalyptus.

Mining, although not a major industry, still occurs in Portugal. Tungsten, uranium, and tin are the most abundant minerals that are mined. Coal and copper are also mined.

TRANSPORTATION

Transportation has seen a huge push in growth in recent years. Portugal's highways are modern and extensive, connecting most areas of the country as well as linking it to Spain. The Metro, a type of subway system, can be found in Lisbon and Porto. This public form of transportation is fast and can carry passengers from one part of the city to another fairly inexpensively.

Seaports and airports are also important centers of transportation for the movement of goods and people through and around Portugal. The thousands of miles of coast in the west of Portugal meant that seaports sprung up early. Today, the most important ports are Lisbon, Porto, Setúbal, and Sines. The three major airports on the continent are in Lisbon, Faro, and Porto.

The islands in the Atlantic also have up-to-date transportation. The seaports in Funchal and Ponta Delgada are important links between the Madeira and Azore islands and the rest of the world. Airports in Funchal, Porto Santo, and Ponta Delgada also bring people to and from the islands.

A TROUBLED ECONOMY

After the recession of 2008–2009, Portugal's economy began to grow again in 2010, but only very slightly (by 1 percent). Then it went downhill again in 2011. Experts predicted that it would be 2013 before Portugal's troubled economy would begin to grow once more.

Meanwhile, Portugal had to request an emergency bailout from the EU and the International Monetary Fund. This was its only hope of dealing with its mountain of debt. The Portuguese government also passed a wave of austerity measures that included increased taxes on gas and electricity, along with cutbacks in the public work force.

Portugal worked hard to do everything that the European Union and the International Monetary Fund asked it to do in exchange for the financial bailout. But the nation has continued to go deeper into debt and its economic situation has grown steadily worse. When Portugal received the EU bailout money, the ratio of its debt to its overall economy, or gross domestic product, was 107 percent—and by 2013, it may reach 118 percent. Experts say that's not necessarily because Portugal's overall debt is growing, but because its economy is shrinking. The Portuguese people, for all their rich culture and history, must find a way to draw on their culture and history if their nation is to survive the challenges of the twenty-first century.

Women doing laundry in the Cavado River

4 PORTUGAL'S PEOPLE AND CULTURE

CHAPTER

Portugal tends to have a **homogeneous** population, although the cities are more ethnically diverse. Most Portuguese are descended from the Celt-Iberians; this group mixed with the Romans and Visigoths who later invaded the area. Only about 4 percent of the population today is made up of immigrants, most of whom are Ukrainians, Brazilians, Cape Verdeans, and

Angolans. The lack of diversity means that most Portuguese people have strong ties, socially and historically, to each other; this has created a rich and interesting culture in Portugal.

THE PORTUGUESE LANGUAGE

Spoken by about 250 million people, Portuguese is the third most spoken European language in the world, following English and Spanish. This is a visible reminder left by the Portuguese empire in its former colonies, in places like Brazil, Angola, Cape Verde, and East Timor.

In Portugal, the overwhelming majority of people speak Portuguese, which is the official language. Many people have been taught Spanish, English, and French, and can speak them fluently, as in many other European countries.

QUICK FACTS: THE PEOPLE OF PORTUGAL

Population: 10,781,459 (July 2012 est.)
Age structure:
   0–14 years: 16.2%
   15–64 years: 65.8%
   65 years and over: 18%
Population growth rate: 0.181% (2012 est.)
Birth rate: 9.76 births/1,000 population (2012 est.)
Death rate: 10.86 deaths/1,000 population (July 2012 est.)
Migration rate: 2.9 migrant(s)/1,000 population (2012 est.)
Infant mortality rate: 4.6 deaths/1,000 live births
Life expectancy at birth:
   total population: 78.7 years
   male: 75.45 years
   female: 82.16 years (2012 est.)
Total fertility rate: 1.51 children born/woman
Religions: Roman Catholic 84.5%, other Christian 2.2%, other 0.3%, unknown 9%, none 3.9% (2001 census)
Languages: Portuguese (official), Mirandese (not official but locally used)
Literacy: 93.3% (2003 est.)

Note: All figures are from 2011 unless otherwise noted.
Source: www.cia.gov, 2012.

RELIGION

Most of Portugal's people are Roman Catholic. Almost 85 percent say they belong to this faith. Protestants make up the largest religious minority, followed by Muslims and Hindus. There are also a tiny number of Jews living in the country.

Despite this lack of religious diversity, Portugal's constitution guarantees its citizens the right to the freedom of religion.

LITERATURE THROUGH THE AGES

Portugal's literature took off during the thirteenth and fourteenth centuries, when troubadours, traveling musicians, and poets spread knowledge throughout the area. In the 1500s, poet Luís

Interior of one of Portugal's many churches.

Typical Portuguese fare

de Camões and **dramatist** Gil Vicente wrote and published several works. De Camões, who wrote the **epic** *The Lusiad*, is celebrated as a national cultural hero today.

Portugal boasts several modern-day writers who have achieved fame. Modern literature includes several poets, including Frenando Pessoa, who wrote during the early 1900s, and writer José Saramago, who won the Nobel Prize for literature in 1998.

The Arts: Music and Architecture

Portugal lays claim to the *fado*, a local form of music unique to the country and often described as sad and melancholy. The songs, of which there are thousands, are said to have come from the music of sailors during the sixteenth century, African slave songs, and Arabic music. Folk dancing sometimes accompanies these fados.

Other types of music are popular as well. Hip Hop Tuga, a type of music that is a mix of pop, African music, and reggae, is listened to by the younger generation.

The architecture that can be found in Portugal's cities, as well as its countryside, is often stunning. The Romans, the Moors, and today's **modernism** all influenced the country's buildings. Portugal is also home to one of the best schools for architecture in the world, the Escola do Porto.

Sports

As in other European countries, the most popular sport in Portugal is soccer (or football, as it's known in Europe). The Portuguese love to play as much as watch. Portugal has excellent teams, ranked third in the world in 2010, and the city of Porto's team has won several world cup titles.

Portugal also has a type of national martial arts, called *Jogo do Pau*, or Portuguese stick combat, since it involves wooden sticks as weapons. The sport originated during medieval times and was used as a style of dueling between young men fighting over a woman. Today, it is a way to celebrate the Portuguese national heritage.

Portuguese Cuisine

The country's close proximity to the sea means that fish and shellfish are a major part of the Portuguese diet. Cod is one of the most widely used fish and is often made into codfish cakes or grilled. Popular foods include grilled sardines (*sardinhas asadas*) and tuna steak (*bife de atúm*).

Child repairing a net

Menus also contain other food grown on Portuguese land, especially potatoes. Perhaps one of the foods most identified with Portugal's cuisine is a custard tart known as a *pastiés de nata*.

Portuguese wines (*vinhos*) are world famous and are enjoyed with meals. Strong coffee is also popular, particularly with dessert.

EDUCATION

Education in Portugal has improved over the past few years, which Portugal's government hoped would lead to an improvement in the economy when there are more educated workers. Right now, the country still has a relatively high **illiteracy rate**.

The current system is divided into *pré-escolar*, which is attended by children younger than six; the *ensino básico*, which children go to for nine years; *ensino secudário*, a three-year level; and ensino superior, made up of universities and polytechnic schools. School is free and **compulsory** for nine years, but more and more people are attending higher-level schools.

Education is hoped to bring about changes in jobs, health care, housing, and other social problems. But with so many young people leaving Portugal to seek opportunities in other countries, the country's future is at risk.

Stormy waters off Portugal's coast

5 PORTUGAL'S FUTURE

Portugal has lots of problems. As it moves toward the future, it will need to find ways to address these. But the situation is not all bad news. In some ways, when it comes to investing in the future, Portugal is way ahead of much of the rest of the world.

What Is Global Climate Change—and Why Are People So Worried About It?

Global climate change has to do with an average increase in the Earth's temperature. Most scientists agree that humans are responsible because of the pollution cars and factories have put into the air.

Global warming is already having serious impacts on humans and the environment in many ways. An increase in global temperatures causes rising sea levels (because of melting of the polar caps) and changes in the amount and pattern of precipitation. These changes may increase the frequency and intensity of extreme weather events, such as floods, droughts, heat waves, hurricanes, and tornados. Other consequences include changes to farms' crop production, species becoming extinct, and an increased spread of disease.

Not all experts agree about climate change, but almost all scientists believe that it is very real. Politicians and the public do not agree, though, on policies to deal with climate change. Changes in the way people live can be expensive, at both the personal and national levels, and not everyone is convinced that taking on these expenses needs to be a priority.

Renewable Energy

Portugal's leaders have made a commitment to reduce their nation's dependence on **fossil fuels**. In 2005, they began an ambitious program to harness the country's wind, rivers, sunlight, and ocean waves. By 2010, nearly 45 percent of all Portugal's' electricity came from **renewable** energy sources. In 2011, the country put into use a national network of charging stations for electric cars, and is developing more electric cars for consumers. Portugal is now on track to reach its goal of using **domestically** produced renewable energy, including large-scale hydropower, for 60 percent of its electricity and 31 percent of its total energy needs by 2020. (Total energy needs include purposes other than generating electricity, like heating homes and powering cars.)

Prime Minister José Sócrates said, "The experience of Portugal shows that it is possible to make these changes in a very short time."

The Portuguese, however, pay nearly twice as much as Americans do for their electricity. (But the United States gets less than 5 percent of its energy from renewable sources.) With Portugal facing such serious economic problems, its energy policy is becoming increasingly **controversial**. But Portugal's leaders are convinced that renewable energy is worth the cost.

And even though Portugal's energy costs are greater than the United States', they're about average for the rest of Europe. Portugal has done a good job at keeping costs down as much as possible by focusing on the cheapest forms of renewable energy—wind and hydropower—while giving incentives to **private** companies to build renewable power plants. The government estimates that the total invest-

These wind turbines in Portugal help to provide the country with a source of renewable electricity.

ment in rebuilding Portugal's energy structure will be about 16.3 billion euros, or $22 billion, but that cost will be borne by the private companies. Once the new plants are up and running, experts predict the system will cost about 1.7 billion euros ($2.3 billion) a year less to run than it did with the old system. What's more, Portugal will be able to export electricity to Spain.

The electricity that comes from natural forces like wind and water can be unpredictable, though. A wind farm that produces 200 megawatts of electricity one hour may produce only 5 megawatts a few hours later when the wind dies down. Solar panels may not do so well on cloudy days, and hydropower may be plentiful during a rainy winter but not during a dry sum-

mer. Meanwhile, people's energy needs are fairly constant.

But Portugal's energy program has found ways to deal with this problem. It has experts who predict the weather, especially wind patterns. They route energy from one part of the **grid** to another as needed. "You need a lot of new skills," said Victor Baptista, the director of the program. "It's a real-time operation, and there are far more decisions to be made—every hour, every second. The objective is to keep the system alive and avoid blackouts."

Portugal's program also combines wind and water. Wind-driven turbines pump water uphill at night, when winds tend to be stronger—and then the water flows downhill by day, generating electricity, when consumer demand is highest.

Portugal's distribution system doesn't just deliver electricity either; it also draws electricity from even the smallest generators, like rooftop solar panels. The government works hard to encourage people to install these rooftop panels. "To make this kind of system work, you have to make a lot of different kinds of deals at the same time," said Carlos Zorrinho, the Portuguese secretary of state for energy and innovation.

Portugal, like the EU as a whole, believes that one of the biggest challenges facing the entire world is global climate change. The economy of every nation in the world depends on the health of our planet in order to thrive. The more nations switch to clean energy sources, the fewer **greenhouse gases** will go into our atmosphere—and the safer will be all our futures.

DANGEROUS DRUGS

In 2001, newspapers around the world carried graphic reports of Portugal's heroin addicts, calling the slums of Lisbon (Portugal's capital city) Europe's "most shameful neighborhood" and its "worst drugs ghetto." The world was shocked by a decision the Portuguese government had made: to decriminalize the personal use and possession of all drugs, including heroin and cocaine. In other words, using drugs is no longer a serious crime in Portugal. The Portuguese police were told not to arrest anyone found taking any kind of drug.

Most of the world thought this was a very bad idea. Newspapers talked about Portugal's "ultraliberal legislation," predicting that Portugal's resorts would soon be flocked with drug tourists. Conservative politicians around the world criticized the new program as being utterly stupid. Some of Portugal's own conservative politicians predicted that planeloads of foreign students would soon be heading to Portugal's beaches to smoke marijuana. Portugal's new PR slogan, they said, should be "Portugal: sun, beaches and any drug you like."

When Portugal decriminalized drugs in 2001, many people feared this would cause an influx of drug tourism—people coming to Portugal

And then the world forgot about Portugal's drug policy. After all, Portugal clearly had bigger problems looming over it. But in 2011, the Cato Institute, an American **think tank**, published a study on Portugal's drug policy. The results were surprising: "none of the nightmare scenarios" initially painted, "from rampant increases in drug usage among the young to the transformation of Lisbon into a haven for 'drug tourists,' has occurred." In fact, "decriminalization has had no adverse effect on drug usage rates in Portugal": instead, these rates "in numerous categories are now among the lowest in the European Union." The study found little evidence of drug tourism, and the level of drug trafficking has also declined. The incidence of other drug-related problems, including sexually transmitted diseases and deaths from drug overdoses, has "decreased dramatically."

Now the world is beginning to once again pay attention to Portugal's drug policy, looking for answers to the drug problems the entire world faces. Drug rehabilitation organizations realized they could find answers for the future in Portugal.

There are widespread misconceptions about the Portuguese approach, says Brendan Hughes of the European Monitoring Centre for Drugs and Drug Addiction, which is based in Portugal. "It is important not to confuse decriminalization with depenalization or legalization," he points out. "Drug use remains illegal in Portugal, and anyone in possession will be stopped by the police, have the drugs confiscated and be sent before a commission."

Guincho Beach on Portugal's coast.

But drug use in Portugal is an administrative offence rather than a criminal one (putting it in the same category as not wearing a seat belt, for example). Drug offenders in Portugal don't end up in the judicial system; instead, they are then sent to special, government-run "dissuasion commissions" run by the government. The police turn over about 7,500 people a year these commissions. Nobody carrying anything considered to be less than a ten-day personal supply of drugs can be arrested, sentenced to jail, or given a criminal record. In Portugal, drug use is considered a health issue rather than a legal issue.

The dissuasion commissions are made up of panels of two or three psychiatrists, social workers, and legal advisers. Their aim is to encourage addicts to undergo treatment and to stop recreational users from falling into addiction. The dissuasion commissions have the power to impose community work and even fines, but punishment is not their main aim.

Portuguese officials are convinced that this policy has encouraged addicts to seek treatment. "Before decriminalization, addicts were afraid to seek treatment because they feared they would be denounced to the police and arrested," says Manuel Cardoso, deputy director of the Institute for Drugs and Drug Addiction, Portugal's main drugs-prevention and drugs-policy agency. "Now they know they will be treated as patients with a problem and not stigmatized as criminals."

The number of addicts registered in drug treatment programs rose from 6,000 in 1999 to over 24,000 in 2008. Portugal now has one of Europe's lowest lifetime usage rates for marijuana. Heroin and other drug abuse has decreased among teenagers, and the percentage of heroin users who inject the drug has also fallen, from 45 percent before decriminalization to 17 percent now. Drug addicts now account for only 20 percent of Portugal's HIV cases, down from 56 percent before the new drug policy. "We no longer have to work under the **paradox** that exists in many countries of providing support and medical care to people the law considers criminals," said Hughes.

Portugal's approach to drug use is changing the shape of the nation's future. It is a note of hope for this troubled nation.

HOPE FOR THE FUTURE

Portugal's **innovative** and aggressive approaches to energy and drugs prove that this nation has the ability to find it own unique solutions to tough problems the entire world faces. Now it needs to put that same innovative and aggressive spirit to work on the other problems that are holding this nation back as it moves into the twenty-first century. If Portugal can do that, with support from the EU, this nation could turn its future around completely, creating better days ahead for the Portuguese people.

TIME LINE

5500 BCE	Fortified villages are established in Tagus Valley.
700 BCE	Celts arrive on Iberian Peninsula.
219 BCE	Romans invade the Iberian Peninsula.
c.400 CE	Visigoths take over Iberia.
711 CE	Moors invade Portugal, and the Golden Age begins.
c.1000	Moors are driven out of peninsula by Christians; Christian Reconquest of the peninsula begins.
1143	Portugal is officially recognized as a country.
1400s	Portugal enters age of expansion.
1539	Court of Inquisition set up.
1580	Spain annexes Portugal.
1640	Portugal regains its independence from Spain.
1812	Sinédrio is set up to spread revolutionary ideas.
1822	Constitutional monarchy is created.
1828	King Miguel I declares the constitution null.
1910	The monarchy is abolished and a democratic republic is established.
1916	Portugal enters World War I.
1926	The military takes over the government, and Salazar becomes dictator.
1939–45	World War II is fought.
1951	The Treaty of Paris forms the foundation of what will become the European Union.
1955	Portugal is admitted to the United Nations.
1957	The Treaties of Rome create the European Economic Community.
1968	Salazar dies.
1974	Caetano is overthrown, and a new democracy is formed; Portuguese colonies are given their independence.
1986	Portugal becomes a member of the European Economic Community.
1992	The Maastricht Treaty creates the European Union.
1999	Portugal joins the European Monetary Union.
2001	Portugal decriminalizes drug use.
2002	Portugal begins to use the euro as its currency.
2005	Portugal begins a clean energy program and totally revamps its energy production.
2008	A global recession spreads around the world, hitting Portugal's economy hard.
2011	A political battle between the Socialist Party and the Socialist Democratic Party divides the nation.

FIND OUT MORE

IN BOOKS

Blauer, Ettagale, and Jason Laure. *Portugal.* New York: Scholastic Library Publishing, 2001.

Hole, Abigail, and Charlotte Beech. *Portugal,* 5th ed. Footscray, Victoria, Australia, 2005.

Luard, Elisabeth. *The Food of Spain and Portugal: A Regional Celebration.* London: Kyle Books, 2005.

Saramago, José. *Journey to Portugal: In Pursuit of Portugal's History and Culture.* New York: Harcourt, 2001.

ON THE INTERNET

Travel Information
www.portugaltravelguide.com

History and Geography
lcweb2.loc.gov/frd/cs/pttoc.html
worldfacts.us/Portugal-geography.htm
www.historyofnations.net/europe/portugal.html

Culture and Festivals
www.2camels.com/festivals/festivals_in_portugal.php3

Economic and Political Information
www.nationmaster.com/country/po/Economy

EU Information
europa.eu.int/

Publisher's note:
The websites listed on this page were active at the time of publication. The publisher is not responsible for websites that have changed their addresses or discontinued operation since the date of publication. The publisher will review and update the website list upon each reprint.

GLOSSARY

annexed: Took over territory and incorporated it into another political entity.

assimilated: Integrated into a larger group in such a manner that differences are minimized or eliminated.

austerity: A government a policy of deficit-cutting, lower spending, and a reduction in the amount of benefits and public services provided.

compulsory: Required.

conservative: Valuing tradition and resistant to change.

contract: Become smaller, shrink.

controversial: Causing arguments and disagreements.

deficit: When spending is greater than income.

deposed: Removed someone from office or from a position of power.

discrimination: Unjust treatment, especially toward people who belong to a different race, gender, or religion.

diversified: Filled with variety, full of many different kinds of things.

domestically: Having to do with something that originates from within the country rather than outside.

dramatist: Someone who writes plays.

economic: Having to do with the production, distribution, and purchase of goods and services.

emigrants: People who leave their homeland and move to another country.

epic: A long narrative.

fossil fuels: Natural fuels, such as coal or gas, formed in the geological past from the remains of living organisms, burned for energy and heating.

greenhouse gases: Greenhouse gases include methane, chlorofluorocarbons, and carbon dioxide, which are put into the air by cars and factories. These gases act as a shield that traps heat in the Earth's atmosphere. The resulting greenhouse gas effect is thought to contribute to global warming and global climate change.

grid: An interconnected network for delivering electricity from suppliers to consumers.

gross domestic product (GDP): The total value of goods and services produced in a country in one year.

hereditary: Passed down, or capable of being passed down, from generation to generation.

heresy: An opinion contrary to church teaching.

homogeneous: Having the same structure or characteristics throughout.

hunter-gatherers: Members of a society whose food is obtained through hunting, fishing, and foraging only.

illiteracy rate: The percentage of a country's population who cannot read and write.

infrastructure: A country's large-scale public works, such as utilities and roads, necessary for economic activity.

innovative: Having to do with new methods and ideas.

liberal: More open to change and a new ideas.

modernism: A cultural movement in the late nineteenth century and early twentieth century that emphasized abstract forms of art over realism.

null: Having no legal validity.

paradox: A seemingly contradictory statement that is nevertheless true.

pension: Income from the government to retired people.

per capita: For each person.

prejudice: An unfair judgment or opinion that's often based on gender, religion, or race.

private: The part of the economy that is not controlled by the government.

progressive: Having to do with new ideas and social reforms.

propaganda: Information or publicity given by a government or organization in support of a doctrine or cause.

renewable: Having to do with energy that comes from natural sources—such as wind, water, and sunlight—that cannot be used up.

republicanism: A belief that a country's power should rest with its voters.

service-based: Having to do with businesses that provides services to customers rather than goods; hospitals, law firms, and tourist resorts are all examples of service-based businesses.

socialist: Having to do with a political and economic theory that advocates that the means of production, distribution, and exchange should be owned or regulated by the community as a whole (the government) rather than by individuals.

think tank: A body of experts providing advice and ideas on specific political or economic problems.

unicameral: Having one house of government.

INDEX

Picture Credits

About the Authors and the Consultant

Authors

Kim Etingoff has written several books for young adults. She lives and works in Boston, Massachusetts.

Shaina Carmel Indovino is a writer and illustrator living in Nesconset, New York.
She graduated from Binghamton University, where she received degrees in sociology and English. Shaina has enjoyed the opportunity to apply both of her fields of study to her writing, and she hopes readers will benefit from taking a look at the countries of the world through more than one perspective.

Series Consultant

Ambassador John Bruton served as Irish Prime Minister from 1994 until 1997. As prime minister, he helped turn Ireland's economy into one of the fastest-growing in the world. He was also involved in the Northern Ireland Peace Process, which led to the 1998 Good Friday Agreement. During his tenure as Ireland's prime minister, he also presided over the European Union presidency in 1996 and helped finalize the Stability and Growth Pact, which governs management of the euro. Before being named the European Commission Head of Delegation in the United States, he was a member of the convention that drafted the European Constitution, signed October 29, 2004.

The European Commission Delegation to the United States represents the interests of the European Union as a whole, much as ambassadors represent their countries' interests to the U.S. government. Matters coming under European Commission authority are negotiated between the commission and the U.S. administration.